INTEGRATIVE PRESENTIMENT

A COLLECTION OF RANDOM THOUGHTS AND STAGES IN LIFE

PRAJWAL SHARMA

Copyright © Prajwal Sharma
All Rights Reserved.

Contents

Contents

Foreword

Integrative Presentiment means combining two or more intuitive feelings about the future and to forge it into something valuable. The book depicts various stages of a person's life and the emotions that gather around. At several stages of life, we often see several scenes and situations that depict presentiment. These situations, along with emotions and depiction, prove to be integrative. Integrative presentiment pinch on that kind of nerve and randomly depict all the scenarios. The scenario are of wide array and many of the readers may perceive or connect with it in their own way.

1. FALSIFIER

The lights with a sharp bloom
Scattered around the soul
Infant blossoming in the womb
Positive mindset is the goal
When hardwork doesn't prove
Everything is doomed to fail
Only thing left is to improve
Inner wisdom is one to avail
We are slave to our desire
Ambition gets a little foggy
Human being is a falsifier
Paved the path but quite snobby
Some little things matter
Time doesn't get wasted
It's time to climb the ladder
In the success we basted

2. PROFOUND

My shadow is dancing
Without you for the first time
The moment be quite entrancing
Feels like a lonely mime
Yesterday I saw something
Your shadow running round
The excitement got me jumping
I am still blind, still profound
Now I am waiting for someone
A person who could still be fun
Bucket list so she could be the one
The era of love has just begun
Tell me the deep seated things
The things you deeply regret
This load will drag your wings
Just free of this extreme debt

3. PEASANTRY

The new couples presently
Makes me wonder sometimes
Tangled like peasantry
No grey between the fine lines
The spark should remain consistent
Doesn't matter when it started
The love must remain persistent
The price shall not be disregarded
Some little things that matter
Not a gift but a gesture
No one likes a slacker
Relationship dives into texture
Roses and rings aren't important
It should always be the bond
The power to be an anger sorbent
To a simple greeting you respond

4. TECHNOLOGY

Made for convience
Yet another innovation
Humans giving lenience
Didn't stop at any station
We walk like a puppet
Aid us the digital string
Lost is our wisdom nugget
Technology is the new king
Devices are somewhat reliable
Do you think about exposure
The advancement maybe liable
Human can't keep it's composure
You seem to go off grid
But you seem so exposed
Technology era is amid
Everything now is superimposed

5. VERSED

Well versed with the concept
Girl power be quite vicious
Success always be onset
The gender in no way pernicious
The role in the society
A mother, a sister or a wife
These notions are propriety
Ambition drives the life
Need a boy, typical stereotype
The ratio tells the story
The target on sight, they snipe
Nothing stops attaining the glory
A deep seated competition
Always keen on proving
This is a near sighted mission
The gender dominance keeps improving

6. UNFATHOMABLE

I was being saved
By my destructive and unfathomable beliefs
From the rebels and den of thieves
All lost and on my knees
I was being mauled
By the burden of society
All the hopes dangled upon us
Notion is denied and not propriety
I was being unfaithful
Not to my loved ones but to myself
Lying were some bizarre indications
Innovative way of being deceitful
I was being hurt
By the constant remarks of a stranger
Clever way of digging the dirt
Avoiding and racing away from danger

7. RAIN

Rain you thief go away
Find another stop to stay
Listening to the sweet song
Staying somewhere I belong
Looting of my possession
Leaving a reasonable impression
The wind blew past the weather
Can bring a couple together
Looting the body heat
Flooding the town street
The clothes comprise of layers
Wasted the talent of ballplayers
Looting the chance to explore
A chance to grow and be more
Making the poor all naked
Destroying the shelter they created

8. SCIENCE

Science is quite elegant
World aided by it's strings
Evidence is quite evident
Humanity blessed with wings
Ladder created for antidote
Innovation will always thrive
Secure way to cast your vote
Science made our race strive
Explaining variety of phenomenon
Answers to the universe mystery
Constituents and it's composition
Mark their place in the history
The fluency and inventions
Explaining all the queries
Magnitude and other dimensions
Answers were told in series

9. PRISTINE

Power defines a nation
Undefiled and unblemished
Clean source is a salvation
Let the resources be replenished
The colossal power of the sun
Pristine and full of potential
Consumption should be done
All facts stated in credentials
Infatuation with unreliable sources
But renewable energy is present
Common man or armed forces
Power and efficiency would augment
A clean source is vital
Our population is profoundly deprived
Breaking this vicious cycle
Reaping the benefits as advertised

10. EVIL

It seems to be unfaithful
Nothing quite unprecedented
It seems to be disdainful
Life shredded and tormented
Everyone has their count
Life is just convulated
The campaign we mount
Evil be heavily populated
Our motive is ambitious
Mission to emerge victorious
Notion is quite auspicious
Please don't make it inglorious

11. TRANQUILITY

Waiting for the moment
Utmost time of tranquility
Presenting us the bestowment
Earning right to tactility
Hard to feel abandoned
Indictment of being in a crowd
Hard for us to be commanded
Strength summoned and endowed
Disguised as a blessing
Everything has a silver lining
Merely means as finessing
Help the person redefining
The wait seems like an eternity
Sweating like the pilchard
Be a part of the fraternity
Free of baggage and filtered

12. SENSATION

Tingling sensation beneath
Something just hurt inside
Reacting to disrespect
Not being oversensitive
Watching ever aspect
Aspiring to thrive ahead
Constantly pulling my strings
Dancing like a puppet
A curve was initiated
Maybe I'll learn something
Walking on a path
Leading to the wrong way
This is a experience
A journey with a tough road
You play with fire
Be prone to be vulnerable

13. FOLLOW YOU

I will follow you
You can drag me to hell
I would hold your hand you knew
In this love I would dwell
I will follow you
Even with a broken heart
Bond is formed, love is a glue
Love for you is off the chart
I will follow you
Your innocence pulls me
I didn't had any clue
Dream of us becoming three
I will follow you
I wouldn't hold my breath
But i realised that you knew
No one shall part us till death

14. EMOTIONS

He has a bottle full of protein
Let his emotions come clean
Alcohol is overrated
Better things are still created
You have better things
Strum those guitar strings
Cry your heart out
Until there is no doubt
Answer lies within you
Stop searching for other clue
You will work it through
Don't join the drunken crew
When you love someone
Fight until there is none
You have to try harder
Be in it with a great ardor

15. WHEN I WAS YOUR MAN

When I was your man
Should have bought you a gift
You invited me in your clan
Then why did we drift
When I was your man
You were quite unpleasant
Living happy was the plan
But you were never present
When I was your man
Maybe I made some mistakes
Being together all that time span
Moving quickly couldn't hit the brakes
When I was you man
Dancing with another stud
Happiness I ran a scan
But i was too deep in that mud

16. ALONE

I am walking all alone
Maybe someone can save me
I should have known
Tried talking no one is free
I am walking all alone
Watching these happy faces
Maybe the chances are blown
Could have gone many places
I am walking all alone
Can you hear your heartbeat
Mind in a restricted zone
Like a diet you don't expect to cheat
I am walking all alone
Seeing her with another man
Emotions were kind of shown
To win her back was my plan

17. POLLY

Sitting on the bench at a corner
No one recognised the foreigner
Her name was polly sherman
Accent sounds a little German
She had a pale skin and red cheeks
Body shaped as sculpted by greeks
Listened to rock and roll all along
The positive vibes were coming strong
She smiled looking some pages
Didn't meet her family for ages
She was on a sketching spree
Looked like a sketch of a tree
She looked at me and smiled
Stared at me and beguiled
She completed it and left the sketch
Sketch was me sitting under obeche

18. LOVE YOURSELF

It's been a long time
Inhibiting myself to climb
Constantly self doubting
Anger on myself keeps spouting
People inducting some shame
I was the only one to blame
People with zero ambition
Laughed at the miserable condition
Zero confidence and denial
Didn't put the person on trial
Antisocial and shyness
Treated a nobody as Your Highness
The lesson set to be learned
Respect has to be earned
The jocks you met in your lifetime
They ain't worth a dime

19. HELP

I was down defeated
Someone please help
Came up with good intentions
Ended up being the sinner
I was always grateful
Someone please help
Pick up the broken pieces
Scattered throughout the floor
I was not ready
Someone please help
Kindly hold on to me
My soul is slowly crumbling
I was not just anyone
Someone please help
Those who came to aid
May you blossom like a cherry

20. EPIPHANY

Something just runs along
Is it just an epiphany
Thinking to myself
Was the hassle worth it
Walking on the rooftop
Foot dangling at an edge
Thinking to myself
Was this an act of courage
Scared to Live normal
Trying to capture my youth
Thinking to myself
Is being old really awful
Always distracting myself
Escaping the actual reality
Thinking to myself
Is my dignity really shielded

21. LADY

Do you feel cold
Lost in desperation
Your choice is bold
No entrance no aeration
I want you to be alive
On this majestic evening
Take you on a long drive
You need to start believing
I am on my way
Please be on time
We need to celebrate your day
Just follow the paradigm
Reached my destination
Crowd was gathered nearby
Message came by the station
Car accident they imply
Analysing the situation
I move past the dense crowd
Got numb for that duration
It was you I cried outloud

22. BETRAYAL

Revelations were quite shocking
Actions took were very provoking
Sins commited cannot be undone
Listening to those things made it spun
Betrayal was a common factor
Roles were played like an actor
Quenching the thirst was the objective
Deception was done as a collective
In this heavenly world was a traitor
Acted sweet but reality was an indicator
Some things are better left unsaid
Some people took things way ahead

23. SPIDER

He dangles like a spider
But only had two legs
He pretends to be an outsider
In the morning making you eggs
His move is out of a book
Alluring, assuring and charming
Try to keep you off the hook
Bad news kind of alarming
He traps you in the web
Like flies he need to feed
Treats himself like a celeb
Gets away with the deed
Clings to you until necessary
Until you feel charmed
If you ask him to marry
Two legged spider would get alarmed

24. DEEDS

They know what you committed
The deed done during winters
Vicious thing you never admitted
The heart exploded in splinters
Maybe it was not enough
The realisation finally struck
Maybe it was just a bluff
The epiphany was pure luck
We knows some secrets
The secrets that are dark
The nights spent sleepless
This might reignite the spark

25. FEELING

I have been waiting
To get out of misery
To soothe my soul
With love and pleasure
Listen to the voices
Deep inside my heart
The name repeats itself
With desire and passion
Something just clicks
A feeling of some kind
The wind drew me away
Didn't take my negativity
Everyday is a new day
New experiences awaits
But noone stands beside
It's you who drives me

26. DAD

Hey dad do you remember
The long stretch of walks
Snowy weather in December
Our long and lengthy talks
Hey dad do you remember
My first day to the school
You stood like a defender
My idol since preschool
I thought I grew old
Responsibility grew past
I thought you couldn't scold
But this will forever last
The journey from a wristwatch
To provision of a better education
Our lifestyle being top notch
This journey left it's initial station

27. DROUGHT

I went to a funeral
Sadness and emptiness
Our count is just a numeral
Adrenaline count as readiness
Like his life's a drought
Dry and a little warm
Oh! he needs a little sprout
To get ahead and charm
Stars twinkle in the sky
Maybe a star is born
Let these birds fly
Before they attempt to scorn
No one skips a phase
Suffering is just eternal
Everyone has their days
Waiting for the next diurnal

28. UNAFFECTED

I am unaffected
when I laid beside you
We must stay connected
oh there is no queue
I am unaffected
when we were young
Positive vibes were directed
kiss used to be minus tongue
I am unaffected
with who should I be
I always neglected
memories under a tree
I am unaffected
what happened to us
Our terms were perfected
never mind here comes the bus

29. PERSPECTIVE

Look yourself in the mirror
Things would become a little clearer
Re analyse your perspective
You will grow and be introspective
You are not less than anyone
Don't hesitate to make that man bun
Think from a positive mindset
Don't make yourself your biggest threat
Don't compare yourself to others
Not strangers nor any brothers
You have a self respect
Don't let it be wrecked
Learn from your mistakes
Achieve greatness whatever it takes
You are a hero of your own story
Be the conqueror find your glory

30. ASTRAY

I pray to God everyday
For an eternal Sunshine
Darkness led me astray
I was searching for a shrine
The dripping of raindrops
Caused a ripple in my heart
A sudden realisation as it stops
Adrenaline pump begin to start
A small and subtle gray matter
Occur between a false word
Truth can cause a major splatter
God can clear the vision blurred
All the truth spoken today
The nature's wisdom radiating
God won't let the foot astray
The one above all is mediating

Acknowledgements

Them that I love, know that I love them. I want to sincerely thank every reader who has stuck with me through this amazing journey and connected with my poetry getting a deep insight into their presentiment.